Alfred Kolleritsch

Selected titles by Alfred Kolleritsch:

Poetry

Einübung in das Vermeidbare (1978)
Im Vorfeld der Augen (1982)
Absturz ins Glück (1983)
Augenlust (1986)
Gegenwege (1991)
Zwei Wege, mehr nicht (1993)
In den Tälern der Welt (1999)
Die Summe der Tage (2001)
Befreiung des Empfindens (2004)
tröstliche parallelen (2006)

Fiction

Die Pfirsichtöter (1972)
Die grüne Seite (1974)
Allemann (1989)

Alfred Kolleritsch

Selected Poems

translated by Iain Galbraith

Shearsman Books
Exeter

Published in the United Kingdom in 2007 by
Shearsman Books Ltd
58 Velwell Road
Exeter EX4 4LD

www.shearsman.com

ISBN-13 978-1-905700-30-1

ISBN-10 1-905700-30-x

Original poems copyright © Literaturverlag Droschl, Graz-Wien, 1978, 1982, 1983, 1986, 1991, 1993, 1999, 2004, 2006; and © Jung und Jung, Salzburg und Wien, 2001.

Translations copyright © Iain Galbraith, 2007.

The right of Iain Galbraith to be identified as the translator of this work has been asserted by him in accordance with the Copyrights, Designs and Patents Act of 1988. All rights reserved. No part of this publication may be reproduced, stored in a retrieval system, transmitted in any form or by any means, electronic, mechanical, photocopying, recording or otherwise, without the prior permission of the publisher.

Acknowledgements
Publication of this book has been made possible by the kind co-operation of the original publishers of most of the poems included here, Literaturverlag Droschl, Graz, as well as the Austrian Cultural Forum, London, which financed the production of the book, and the State of Styria (Das Land Steiermark), which financed the translations. We are grateful to all of these organisations for their assistance in this project.

The cover shows an untitled oil painting by Hartmut Urban. We are indebted to the artist's estate, and the owner of the painting, for their permission to reproduce it here. The photograph of the painting is by Petra Schober.

CONTENTS

from: *Einübung in das Vermeidbare*
(Studying the Avoidable, 1978)

> I don't trust what comes to mind . . .   11
> What is experience . . .   12
> Since then it has all been quite different . . .   14
> When a person writes . . .   15
> The house is locked up . . .   16

from: *Im Vorfeld der Augen*
(In the Forecourt of the Eyes, 1982)

> . . . so there is a boundary . . .   17
> The hill was inside us . . .   18
> The eye outgrows . . .   19
> Why go on shovelling . . .   20
> There are days when things . . .   22
> "Never again" – that was a phrase . . .   23
> The sounds are exhausted . . .   24

from: *Absturz ins Glück*
(Nosedive to Happiness, 1983)

> Analogy   25
> Peace   26

from: *Augenlust*
(Eyes' Delight, 1986)

> Paean after René Char   27
> Unrest of Its Own Kind   28
> But How Can This Be Man?   29
> Now Here   30
> Creation   31
> Seventh Question   32
> Against the Elevated Tone   33

Transcending	35
Death Piece	36

from: *Gegenwege*
(Opposing Paths, 1991)

Crush	37
Place	38
Man	40
Island	41
When?	42
Fragment	43
Against Completion	44
Colour Is Slough of Things	45
For Zoë	46
Once	47
In View	48
Hope	49
Difference	50
Tuscany, Storm	51
For P. H.	53
Blossom First	54

from: *Zwei Wege, mehr nicht*
(Two Paths, Nothing Else, 1993)

Idyll	55
Departure	56
No Path	57
Thus Together	58
Strange	59
Tautology	60
Two Ways	61
That we are not it . . .	62

from: *In den Tälern der Welt*
(In the Valleys of the World, 1999)

    On What Remains   63
    The Circle   64
    Into Uncertainty   66
    Harvest   67
    Unrest   68
    On the Pictures 1   69
    On the Pictures 2   70

from: *Die Summe der Tage*
(Sum of the Days, 2001)

    Boundaries   71
    On Asking/Answering   72
    Voice   73
    "That Mysterious Yearning toward the Chasm"   75
    Immersed   76
    Arguing with Parmenides   77
    Song   78

from: *Befreiung des Empfindens*
(The Liberation of Feeling, 2004)

    You approach . . .   79
    Who is this departure meant for . . .   80
    The unsurpassable . . .   81
    Out of the lake the fountain . . .   82
    I have brought fruit . . .   83
    She stretches her life . . .   84
    To live . . .   85
    Overreach your outward gaze . . .   86
    Gentleness Paraphrases Itself   87
    Intimations   88
    This is the pain . . .   89
    We have gazed ourselves free . . .   90
    When I see her I know . . .   91
    Result   92

from: *tröstliche parallelen*
(comforting parallels, 2006)

    When from the grey of the evening . . .   93
    The coat of mail, closeness . . .   94
    Far we went . . .   95
    He sifted through himself . . .   96
    Narrated into the poem . . .   97
    While changing . . .   98
    To wreak havoc as the clouds do . . .   99
    I kept . . .   100
    Conspicuous   101
    Uplifted by writing . . .   102
    "It Rounds"   103
    Addressed by the wind . . .   104

Uncollected (2007)

For Hartmut Urban   105

Biographical Notes   107

Selected Poems

I don't trust what comes to mind . . .

I don't trust what comes to mind.
There was a time I'd sit there
with a caved-in rib-cage
and something starting to bark: boiling anger,
a tendency to moan
and those big, protruding ears.

These days
I search for tracks,
leaves crushed underfoot,
someone with failings
who will torment me
and, when I show up,
without looking up,
keep on gluing the lid of a box.

Sure,
I can't get used to this;
I notice
habits are what I don't have.
Yesterday's interior was a borrowed thing;
things outside are all in their places;
now someone is pouring out poetry –
an opportunity squandered.

I tell myself:
you liked the heavy eyelids better,
found finding more appealing
than searching,
the ready-made meal
more agreeable than hunger.

What is experience . . .

What is experience
(the eyes are beggars),
two hands open?

Dogs' backs approaching –
there's the smell of moisture,
an oily blot
startling the dusty street.

We take a look
and have taken a look:
the bark is no longer shedding.

A dried frog lasts,
flies are lying everywhere;
we slog it through the light,
a pathetic brow flap
protecting the memory.

"I can't see you."
"I'm here!"
"There's nothing there."
Why do we look behind things?

"Mao Tse Tung too saw the essence"
appear, the transformation,
the idea, a universal,
everyone's tube for close viewing,
the summary,
the destruction of "first sight".

And then: anything with a grip on itself
puts itself to use –
the essence pulls back the curtains

and blabbers about necessity,
the movable tragedy.

The immovable riff-raff of the antithesis
needs a different stage: there are other roles now.
The eyes go on making good headway
till the Earth feels the shame.

Since then it has all been quite different . . .

Since then it has all been quite different.
I have taken a step beyond myself.
I stood and watched the rainy day.

I am not going to cry.
To live on a building site
between barrows, sacks and duckboards –
protected, for once, by caterpillars and buckets!

I have a house and am walled in;
I have a picture on the wall,
a cross-section of the brain-stem.
It looks like Josef Stalin;
his moustache is gloomy,
more threatening than his fists.

You showed me the obit.
I stroked your hair into your face.
During the night I told you: there,
behind that window, is where my father died.

I am remote, too remote.
Take this shiny bit of steel
and stave in the walls.

When a person writes . . .

When a person writes
the doors won't close,
one question sticks to another,
one anxiety turns out
the next.

Harmony will keep breaking through
like ice spreading through steel
and the ubiquitous sense
of warm drizzle.

Then your eyes smart,
then you kill the thing you love,
then kindness turns to a stranglehold,
then you write your way into the void
or say:
"Only to the edge of the heart".

It's what's being said to you,
with only one hand
to hide behind.

The house is locked up . . .

The house is locked up.
The windows and doors are deaf.
The flowers on the walls
climb higher every day.
Soon the house will be overgrown
with sprays of blossom.
The scents will be strong,
the colours denser than silence.

Behind them the house, bidding
us forget, leaving our thoughts
to the void that fills
with names. They are tied up
under a torrent of knots,
never to be severed.
Nobody knows what the flowers are called.

Parting has brought the aloofness
of early prosperity, of a startled
untouchable spring, keeping
the old inhabitants out. Round and round
they walk, shading their eyes,
the path they tread growing deeper,
its soft walls rising ever higher.

Such is the dauntless power of beauty
to take its leave and go, the power to conceal.
Behind our backs, the snowfall
fills our tracks. The sky trickles.
The hot light that once fell
through the windows, the wind above the door –
they suffocate, deep beneath the flowers.

. . . so there is a boundary . . .

. . . so there is a boundary:
what has been said is a boundary.

The piece made of words
I cannot call mine
to the end.

Is it for others then?
One must not steal an ear.

The echo
turns up for the lesson.
If it is ice
it will be the flower
that returns.

"You are giving us the lesson now",
you opined,
"such is your horrendous facility".

How monstrous statements are.
One word
put to death by another,
re-routed to the answer
of who it's for,
dragged ashore for the sake of a truth
that has long since left
these shores.

The hill was inside us . . .

The hill was inside us.
Two slopes bore its gradient,
the sky above
already pulling you away.

Of course
what once was
had now caught us up.

Indisputably,
that moment
has melted into the earth;
it need never feel
hunted.

Gravity
is without law.
The grass blades barely bend,
the wind keeps
us still.

The eye outgrows . . .

The eye outgrows
the height
that carries it.

The bearish head
is full of *land*.
Tendrils
catch the light.

Even in the haze
one edge slides
towards the other –
and all is colour.

Why go on shovelling . . .

Why go on shovelling
whatever the eye scoops up
back into sentences
and giving things that litany
about existing?

Out of milk jugs, flower-pots,
Agaves, armchairs, parasols,
rafters, fences and clover-blow
grows the madness
we manage.

And that inextinguishable love –
the one who was unique.

Ants disappear into the cracks,
wild goings-on
along the walls,
as if the gods yet again
had a hand (?) in it.

As for the fragrance hereabouts –
we barely have a word for it!

"The world is a picture
of the world *we* need",
the heart: a fin
for the relentlessness of death,
us as marks thereon,
meek with truth.

Then there is you, your hair
trailing the wind. You are gone.
The amniotic fluid drains
with every word.

What a delight
they should break these bonds.

There are days when things . . .

There are days when things
are the names of things,
characters
written beneath the sky,
deployed by the tellers of tales.

A flag of ice rules the day,
death's other face,
the law.

That is when you are away.
Measured against this parting
no measure fits.

"Never again" – that was a phrase . . .

"Never again" – that was a phrase
for some final day in the year,
as if it were possible
not to be the one
who was going to live with the rest
of this great life.

Often, as if through a hedge,
comes the echo
without the voice disguised:
fatal encouragement
to accompany to putrescence
that dead apple in the hip.

The sounds are exhausted . . .

The sounds are exhausted.
They enter the scene marching in goosestep:
recollections of fear, hazard and distress.

The half-open door
does not impinge on our space.
Air streams past us.
The generations and melting ice
hope for future vaults.

The time has come again
to experience, to abandon oneself
with the arrogance of these colours:
to be oneself,
freeing oneself for THINGS.

To turn out with our stillness,
you say,
is to find our lost abyss,
the austere golgotha.

Now we are here, what place is this?
Where will the whole world be
when we end?

The point is to find a way out
of this complacent gravitas,
these divinations.

Beginning and end will no longer be the measure
when one's own heart
knows its name:
we are here to be that name.

Analogy

In the snow, the mountains
over which you *walked*;
that was a path, you think,
because you *walked*.

I feel closer to you
when I take our tracks further,
saying the valleys
in the mountains are too dark,
lacking your brightness –
but you are quite understood.

Allow me these secondary images;
they come closer
to what I can't say:
the broad road
with the glorious sky standing beside it
is closed;
you not being here
is the cloth
that does not clothe.

We show each other
our similar pains:
the way you, found again
in my hands, ceased to be.
Freezing to death.

Peace

The fact that it occurs to us
to imagine going home:
what we are leaving we know.

To stand in the rubble,
torturing one's back
in order to touch:
can she know what we need?

The knife's fortune in splitting us apart,
the leap it prompts
increasing our vulnerability:
the desert doesn't work,
nor does the mortar
that keeps us together.

What remains is a thought, the eye
blinking, a petal's life long.
Writing on the wall
calling itself home
replaces the verifiability
of home's existence.
No intervention can make it happen.
Wherever the journey goes
it reaches the dead –
no, not even that.

Paean after René Char

"You alone, wild leaves, fulfil your lives",
ours are lost, belonging to the hand,
the owned world that helps itself, the chains.

You are of the earth, of different growth;
where you meet, you more untouched,
your daily round is the long term,
appearance, great variety.

Whirling leaves, your withering
does not renounce one thing within another;
you are where things come together –
tranquillity and storm,
winter and summer,
day and night,
"igniting in moderation".

To throw us off centre
you rush, we fall badly;
wrongly used
we trade eternity in,
false history,
and are murdered.

You are the dance on all sides,
through us and out of us;
you replace us with your peregrinations
which we can't follow.

Imagine this without us.

Unrest of Its Own Kind

Extended this far: as a body.
Space needs a boundary
wherein each world talks
and plays and gives its sequel
(to the gods and machines).

It stretches its arms beyond "itself"
and the birds fly with it. The field
it is walking in comes to meet it
(the name death has proved best for this).

You tell me this and say: this is the step
it can walk over, whose places
are all its places
and also the fall –
in hatred and misery, lying, war
and the conjunction of beautiful desire and beauty.

What the body suffers and what it gives,
between these two is nothing dark;
the nocturnal surroundings
draw our escape on a short route
(to which you would grant no truth).

But How Can This Be Man?

Night in the fissures of speech
keeps silent, aside, outwith visibility.
All the remainder is name

and reverses nothing. Set just so,
it is overrated by the light;
it tears off mouthfuls become flesh;
the world's heads roll.

The throats are bloody. The gate
has subsided. The breast
sings its song. The outward plunge
has assumed its position: unhappy freeze.

The wanderer, with his loss sent ahead
to wait, his shadow preserved:
the delight of his eye eclipses him,
it punishes ancient experience,

the exposed, what is grown painless,
the well-ordered scum, the images.
It abandons all the world, sets locks breaking,
astonished in its desire for things other.

Now Here

Sunlight in the room,
a flower remains,
a hand searching
for the history of the others.
Time will take us there.
Its sole pretence.

Creation

The body wants the world;
through it run furrows,

torn tracks
walking it.

Enticed to see,
the eye tries
the opened sky.
Flights of clouds
display space.

They multiply the senses,
hastening the body
to accept visibility.

This encounter.

Seventh Question

Have at last stepped out of the house.
The first step out, the house is gone;
it never was a house; doubt
it was, wanting to settle itself.

The trees stand fast (like stones,
the eyes, sick, seek some comparison,
yearning for peace, to stay upright,
digging their claws into what they can see)

outside: hands dash up to my face.
The second step, moving away,
loses the first track, the track is gone:
grounds for measuring the way, holding
in points of view; the stride swings away,
distance catching the steady stance off guard,
testing what is narrow, whatever waiting sets up.
Distance collects things, takes them in:
the evening light, parting, the remains of a sun –
there and when back? The eyes hurt.

What is *ahead* is what causes the hurt:
the world, the other house, the tall
wind that sweeps, frees, lays down the light.
Then that long time before each step:
to be close to the place from which the road meets
the sloes, alders, beetles, flies, butterflies,
kites, oaks, pine forests, sponges,
grey grass, stones, feathers, stunted birches,
jays, autumn crocuses, switches, briars, droplets,
clouds, currents, stubble fields –

your hands will open if you follow the furrows,
your ability to see, soothings, step by step.

Against the Elevated Tone

"Yet much is done better by the cool of the night":
when the eye is freer and reaches for you.

You are here. Between us is the place expanding the meeting,
a space made by night, a terrain for us, likewise for all.

The wind pushes moon and stars together, the cliffs, soil, woods,
love torn out, rising toward you, out there with you:

"I" – the lust of experience, a cry that wants us,
the narrows noisily pushing away, the net tearing, ground

flowing from us clod by clod, the sphere becoming night air.
We are the leaf-sounds, drawn into each other, the wanderers.

Unseen, light, shell-less, we are whatever place surrounds us,
the soil and the tracks, we are of the world, happening,

joyful, with exorbitant eyes, sans countenance, without wall
    or shadow
to define our bodies, our desire an owl on the wing.

(Whoever it encounters inhabits its closeness, whoever it loses
night protects – a night that is colder, further from the "difficult",
averted and more lovely than armour-clad light, than muscle's
    obdurate
submersion of life. Duration of obduracy as the duration of
    a day.)

You are the voice, flitting to mine, displaced into hearing; hissing
the ear absorbs things less fleeting. Air boils over.
Memory slides up, layer by layer, from open arms
comes the future, once in the bushes, now turning above the
    hills,

turning *again* while names exist, gashes made in the flesh. The names
retain what "rustles and roars" not, coming to us (love?),

what hangs high in clouds, not evading the stone, whatever is mute.
Nests are broody with death, to spite the reasons, to spite the splendour,

the moisture blearing and trickling in us, and into our desire.
Desires are our movements, skin to skin, and the fervency of the boundary.

Heat! and heat is blind and does not freeze: it does not want
to have seen. That glowing/appearing that beguiles you and me,
forcing *us* down, has missed us. And we do not talk about talk
(draining words does not purge the ground). I hear

your resistance, you who will not see. "Not consciousness",
   you say, "arousal",
you say, "and *there* is where our home is, before light, search with me,

take what is massy, and lost, and empty, so that nothing
may have the right to set a trope of the world above the world."

Transcending

They are one,
gums, teeth, lips
and the red salmon.

Biting, you succumb to the temptation
to transfer – to translate
their resistance into taste,
the world flooding the senses.

"Pepper on the mid-tongue,
implacable, melted
into silky butter – not to be told apart
once they blend", say you,
"hot, salt and mellow sour."

I watch the conversion, evident
in the play of your cheek muscles from the moment
when thought has entered the dish and
what you've been promised, beyond the ingredients,
is what's new: evanescent and repeated
at the second bite (persistent in its lasting).

This pleasure moves you and you are party:
in the manner that pain is also everybody's pain.
Tasting takes you aside.

With it you drink wine like the wind. The rest
of the oyster sauce is a triumph in your eyes;
so simple, with us, all that *is*.

Death Piece

Things left that since have stayed
as they were: each for each,
the green bottle, spices, bread,
the glasses, the cured meat,
the oil a murky green.

The woman is dead. I see her death.
Everything here is that death,
this worn threshold is death.
Through the window: light. Through something windowless
the woman flitted (before she took her rest).
Whoever enters this room, enters death.

The garden is overgrowing. What once was hers
is impoverished, bent back on itself,
without her hand a remnant,
deserted by the eye, an heirloom,
shamelessly made over.
The happiness of newcomers was her burden.

The flies are loyal still.
They buzz a circle round her empty space.
The place is collapsing, what is left
shifting from light to shade;
more earth takes from the sky
what she directed towards it.

Crush

The torn skin: in the afternoon
the hot window, behind it you;
before that a long cut, the tune,
the infinite cut at the end;

too alone now to be merely alone;
the bridge spanned from the books
to the emptied glass, writing
leaping off, in the face of the gaze;

the table standing there, the chairs,
all we sat out and dammed up
in the scuffed cover of the bench –
all these signs that bodies were here,

soft skin. Into the room marches
Bing Crosby, his coat slung over his arm,
with him the writers, rivals
in vulnerability, their flaws and bruises.

Their immeasurable memory
is the sojourn, the breath taken in the margins,
blowing down walls for admission
that has no threshold, no you;

the sun stays, the whole crush finds its way here;
mountains and trees, touched,
show willing; the glasses shiver;
word and wine concede his objection,

uttered and gainsaying, henceforth
perceptible, what is lost losing;
cigarette ash plays death,
three rooms, graves, a song too, luck.

Place

The gaze that carries to the roofs,
following the soot, the rain,
the snow, the light,
still awake with the night,
has the sky above it
down to the back yard.
He sees the town blocked out,
the empty square,
as if what lay beyond were disgust,
flesh congealed to a face.

The oceanic is only here
to hallow the place – protective magic;
the hole torn by thinking gapes;
tended as "holy" it is kept well apart
from whatever sedates or wounds.

The hours of difference
(clock hands in advance free fall
coming full circle)
push off; in this small space,
moving to the books and pictures
music is time;
its path, cleansed of abodes,
passes through the hearts of children
and the children dance to its closeness.

Friends have disappeared, meetings
gone by the board, qualities become repellent,
traps snapping shut,
disloyal to the unrecognized and to memory;
the equinox of life and death has unmingled,
the rattle of the end is heard
in the wall, and the warmth protects.

When you leave the house
as if walking in photographs
visibility is spellbound,
occupied in advance. Screamed at
by sameness one ducks away; all things being earth
and returning to earth is a waste;
the game is exposed
and still at it; those who hide
enjoy; what goes down overexcites itself,
staggers with reason, lies, searches for the truth
and loves, is defenceless,
is real.

Crushed in one's fist, extinguished
for the eyes, far from the ear,
something possible hurts
and continues to let us be.

Man

Alone, but the hand is there;
it holds him fast (still it)
and makes the gazes, worn-out, shine;
breath flies, closing in now
comes the meeting itself;

behind closed
eyes out there in the world
we are here, who know little,
who are where it takes us,
butterflies launched from the fingers,
duped into appearance,

multiplied, mercilessly begot,
the hand leading us home to what was;
come to nothing, the body gives
what as a body it cannot give;

it is when it falls that it
rolls on its side in the grave,
burying with it the signs.

Island

No love penetrates the briars.
The thicket belongs to the thorns.
One blossom covers the next
until the sun burns them out.

No gaze ever fills.
What eyeballs the gaze
becomes darker at every glance,
draining it by terror.

The regions of the bow
drift past one another.
The tone grows silent; the oils
of plants lose their fragrance;

the words remind us of little;
nobody gives any backing;
high and low tide play at time
and the sea and the sun and.

The protecting hand does not stir.

When?

When there is one
who slips inside our voice
and wakes within our eye,
listening, saying yes,
let us hear, let us see,

when he is here,
in our marrow,
dying with us, easing death,
love will be
that safe existence –
two against one.

If sentences threw sparks,
being more enlightened, would our experience
prove more peaceful, would proving prove self-evident?

Our faltering, sheltered by its own path,
would head for the end: to find
what cannot be without being found.

Fragment

"Mistaken am I, come down"
as the reed, overgrown,
I kill the riverbank,
the parting,
of the mud
I wade
with divers creatures
in my breast,
rats' nests,
not-at-home snakes:
as if for protection

the stars above, holy school
of the night,
their waves,
they tear the mirror,
their scintillation
ruffles me,
the picture emerges
or does not;

never in all this misfortune,
not even for the grasses,
does a single thought keep;
before its hour has come
the wind spirits it away;

grown younger for death,
icily blowing as it ages,
the heart
goes to its grasses,
sinking towards
the indefinite pond,
nor does it help the water

"as for us, who,
so that",

Against Completion

Ripped from the body,
one part, the sacrifice,
meant for the sun: your gaze –
to be in the head, released, released
from this history of limbs –

joining grief
to the death-piece memory.
In it things get ensnarled
with no intention
of supporting the feed of light.

Its being your gaze too –
to what possible end?

Colour Is Slough of Things

Colour is slough of things,
streaming to the pored eyes
what belongs to the world
while the world belongs to the eyes,

and all things in turn
have no abiding in themselves;

the most beautiful hovers
and nothing is there
to face it –

it swirls round us here
and swirls away,
the poverty of the forked tongue
that holds fast

and talks, as if day and night
did not belong together.

For Zoë

You were out on the hill
that summer's day
and all around was pointing away
to wind and light instreaming –

apple trees, heavy with growth
standing on the slope, a cat,
like you, stretched in the grass,
your back, more than ready,
rising to pleasure us both –

the cornfield stood by us too,
its green turning sky to blue
and scent of flowers scenting you –

and all our words were gone,
while what held us was invisibly close,
palpable in you as a thought, beginning,
empty, holding us back
and carrying us away.

Once

Once we were the light in the orb,
a ray-burst, an image, the distance
between beginning and end, their plaything,
every sunbeam that struck us
exaggerating us for bigger suns.

Memory sent birds in advance,
burning feathers the wind; you wrote
on red paper how you loved
what was dark; you brought in the end;
the orb foundered, the power
of thought against the privilege of death.
On the stage in front, ragged as knowledge
with the light in its fist, death was
death in the opera, love
da capo love, the prescribed decoy.

The red knight has turned, with the
blood in the snow unseen, no pain,
all things made equal; the dead knight
in the tree, forsaken by the terror
which preserved him, proclaims the dark.

In View

Above the clouds or below the clouds
things head for the end –
ahead
and centuries
if one counts.

In the meadows, fields,
roads,
as the presence of a voice,
fire writes
a towering
mountain.

The beginning wants things passing,
the view longer
before the day.

Hope

The fire between two glances –
as you stand in the blaze
counting the years
burning away
is it likely anyone will come along
and put out the fire,
braiding his wreath,
telling the tale?

Difference

To live
so that living is for the dead,
their manger
running straight through your sleep,
their watering trough of ice.

The trees are half-size;
the level of grief
invokes memory;
it is family trees
warrant the invocation.

Whoever receives the grief
receives life;
Eurydice walks before him
slipping off experience's glove,

its claws as filthy
as awakening;
return babbles death,
outwitting separation
with half-open eyes.

Tuscany, Storm

The open raining, water-weals
catching the village off guard,

pines and oaks
changing veils,

lightening splitting the hills,
wine country catching the thunder,

and leaves whirling green,
rippling colours rustling;

the statues, rusty-brown, dance,
the garden as astonished as the wind,

droplets spraying through cracks,
people taken into the barn;

the centre tears, its singularity
wincing in the parting,

the countryside rages down,
confusion on every side;

the fact that the country exists,
says the country, is the abyss,

the fact of appearance at all,
with the sun fetching the light,

creating the eye and the roses
and coming back with the wine;

so the rain gives a perpendicular,
the decline, the sky and earth,

the ascent of the mist;
and how threateningly all space grows,

with the sea over the roofs
robbing the birds of their flight,

dolphin and swallow
merging at the eye;

the exchange-song rings in the ear
alongside the grumbling,

lasting into waiting, until it passes
(into memory? into the open?)

For P. H.

"As the sweet apple reddens on the highest branch"
so gleams the snow around it,
the branches lowering dark and bare
against the glare of the sun.

It is your apple, frozen,
glowing, the very last,
dug into growth,
freed for resurrection in others,
giving us this moment
in which the moment is felt.

What could be more visible?
Snow burns out the eyes;
the wound draws a circle around what we see,
wherein everything else may vanish.

Blossom First

The compulsion to speak
which makes
the apple-tree bud
is the fear
of encountering gardens,
grey rows
year after year.

The tongue swells
in the eyes,
a word tugs,
cutting its enclosure
in the great gazing

which flowering
had bloomed ahead of,
far ahead, and was therefore
now returning
whence
experience loves us,

for whom even in flowering
a being is thrown free,
his fragrance also, affected,
overwhelmed with it
to the point of silence.

That the garden
be even the whole of life?
So dreadfully different
from what other things are,
and alike?

Idyll

We found nothing
to be lived as it was,
or there was nothing
as it was.
We read the obituaries
but even that grief
was not grief.
We were the mask
and the feeling allowed it
in order to spite the cold,
chilling in its destruction
of what had never been. We went along,
glad of the blood,
the fragments, the incisions.
Ghosts bled,
lust for the abysmal
spiralling into paradise,
and we paying murders in exchange,
each for each.
The connections were discussed
by the connections,
not by the things, not by us.

Departure

The steps have been neatly swept
to a path
and already the birds draw
horizons, the distant forests wait.
What do the fields hold for us?

But the houses are inaccessible,
their deep gardens
not to be measured
between one arm and others;
what has grown
in these gardens tells lies.

We leave
with the clouds
as if they harboured signs;
things we love
leave their traces –

perhaps that crooked twig
in the village? Wherever they have space
to wait, to drink,
to be grateful without shame
to the stones, their hardness,
to stand in the wind
or under the red sky
without ever having arrived.

No Path

When the one word is missing
one cannot utter
that links the other words,
redistributing them along itself,
straying from its kind,
the world passes
into sentences,
nets stringing together,
knotted, so
forgetting the uncatchable,
that other water;

leaning on divers things
we pass one another
downstream,
exchanging lies,
our truth,
and wherever there are fields,
frozen empty,
the frost feeds us
its message:
a single whiteness
lighting up our pupils,
one of its stars
piercing our foreheads;

but even this silence
is not an experience.

Thus Together

It is said
that we are with words,
speaking what is,
hearing phrases of looking,
and that we have our yes in touch,

in this one,
which belongs to itself
as does desire
in other bodies:

the square
that will not be silent
whirring upwards with beating wings
again and again,
creating the boundary

with no centre.

Strange

The grey, the immortal grey
of pigeons
swelling up to their sameness,
one flight stuck to the next,
one note squatting next to the other,
cooing, hazy,
their flight fouling the sky.

Pecking at the masonry,
addicted to lime, they transform
whatever gives them a foothold
into themselves, gorging,
stolid racers making a break,
single-minded, clouds,

smug chunks of words,
recoiling,
excreting their monotony,
their caustic, that levelling caustic;

soft-haired they hover,
damned souls, peaceless
flutterers over water,
deceivers of placidity,

of the spirit.

Tautology

Every phrase, jammed into the line,
rotting into script,
adds to the account
of our being alone on the slope.

Two Ways

Water divided into two streams,
cut
for the border through them,
separated for touch,
the most uncertain,
loved by two organs,
folded into each other,
torn apart
for so little between,
for their double head,
for the explicatory and the perplexing;

two hands digging to the left and right,
day and night, without antagonism,
but two lungs breathing
along two riverbanks,
water and ice,
on experience and experience itself,
two roots belonging to one earth,
then two roses, two names fighting,
painfully together, inimical,
two birds distance-bound,
making for withdrawal,
"to pass over and return"
beyond the most separate mountains.
One double-mirrored,
with sunken spirits and double-horned
a longing blasts the day
and the air glows with hatred
that orders things
as if nothing had happened,
as if *one* herb could heal all our days.
And in both corners sits death.
Two ways, nothing else.

That we are not it . . .

That we are not it,
not us,
and somehow instead
the light
and these pastures,

as a gift,
as a parting.

On What Remains

Parting quickens, ripening is blessed,
death begins its story; colours
are never lovelier. It takes its path.

Its name: autumn. The murmur
of the fruits striving into life;
how it loves that boundary.

It is abundance, its name disappears,
bringing looking, being looked at.
Such is its rapture, it overflows.

It draws us in; gathering in thousands,
we are witnesses; it is the season's rule
to show oneself and disappear.

Blows of change, the abyss, living
to die. The harvest brims over. Change
and life overdoing desire: beauty.

Shredded into colour; in this form
closeness withdraws, the paths
walk home, the turns are gone.

Exuberance everywhere; what heads
for the end wears the lustre of the mask.
The wine ferments. Thus memory begins.

It retains the bright air – so limpid
that longing perseveres.
The gaze is a vastness.

For Peter Horst Neumann

The Circle

The leap
beyond repetition
into the pathless zone –
into the undisclosed (thus foliage
on the way to Mycenae lay hidden in the haze) –
was no return, no first things
lowered in the shadows;
there was no thing one might wake
from slumber; words
flapped about quite empty.

The wilderness grows
around us unprotected; now
towns are going wrong,
the sea festering; no spade,
no net finds
legible traces; without reason
things are one with themselves.

Music starts up, swarms of bees
bear history, cooling
and staying put. Notes, chimes of bells
nurtured by decay, perforate
the continuum; fire burns,
quartets arising and perishing
in the ear, variations,
fast redemptions. What
a sacrifice. Marilyn Monroe's life-size
at the Coronado Hotel, condemned
to be past, but deathless.

The plain all around us is a circle,
tracks dissolving in the snow;
life's clouds, frayed out in the sky
and then these hills where we can stop by,

with nothing outside, no end, no beginning
when the One is
visible as wine. Radiant peace,
no sooner found than gone.

Into Uncertainty

He takes the path,
he no longer takes the path, he speaks it;
he cannot speak it;
a sky is there
that lacks a heaven,
and animals creep up,
invisible,
without extension –
intangible magnitudes:
and the lack of words
crumples the images,
no letter
wanting the other,
spinning from the bird-shelters
so the flashing birds
are not birds,
an aria, unvoiced,
is as far from the head
as once were gazing and love.
If the pond did not exist,
collecting water,
its mirror for the duration of a breath –
and the poppy has blossomed,
the oak rotted, yellow foam
swallowing its bark, life
resurgent stolen from non-life.
Whatever exists goes to extremes,
spilling the seed: its cursèd
intercourse with identity.
The neighbour has left, the child overslept,
the threshold broken: that un-word
closeness. The fact that the fire has burned
cannot vindicate the ash.
Scattered on the sea
he walked out to sea.

Harvest

He stands beneath the apple tree;
red balls marvel
at autumn leaves; why should apples
fear the winter
who learn to freeze,
gleaming and rotten.

To be here with a hand.
Their falling finds us out,
making us listen to the black seeds.
To whatever ripeness provokes.

Unrest

To go out in the rain
into the wide-open country
away from the forests
from the shelter of ringing leaves
from the water talk –
to forget
all that is salvaged, its sameness,
deadlocked in brackets,
with the houses in view, windowless;
thing-tired, foreign to all expectation.

On The Pictures 1

These pictures
which threw you into the world,
are added to the earth.

(Like countless thousands of others,
but how few are they?)

How can we not feel
ashamed of our eyes!
Displaced from childhood,
pieces on a board,
without news,
without the flight of birds –
without nests, bushes.

No one, fearing death
from mushrooms,
is transported
by the glitter of stone.
Deep and steaming
was the sludge
of your colours.

Blank now, in a passe-partout –
memory,
and this shudder.

For Hartmut Urban

On The Pictures 2

He is alone with his fragment,
exposed, and has sunk
into thicker lips,
addressed by their derision,
their stone's throw to beyond.

This has given him the world,
nothing more, play
in sight of the cohorts of rules.
What came to mind was his pain.

He coalesced with things lost;
gleaming with night sweat
he understood
the din in his ears,
he alone.

His utterance of names
was denied by the names themselves;
he became the answer,
finally the riddle.

For Hartmut Urban

Boundaries

The garden shamelessly open –
our gaze touching
herbs, weeds,
the peach tree, confused,
grown wild;
beyond lie green giants, hulks of willows,
oak stumps. Mistletoe kills.

You in the midst of all this, lost,
mad with repetition
for days
that have blacked themselves out in the branches.

Everything has your name; bestower of names
you have entered thorns to the language
and camellias, the flowers
that look like your hands.
Every petal is a note
in the melody played for flies.
Kingfishers plunge from the hedges.
Herons pass over the house;
they are carrying away what we shall miss:
agility, the delicate fin,
gills and breathing.

The garden gate shuts fast.

On Asking/Answering

1
Language
bursts open
like a seed pod
wanting the answer –
which you don't give.

The answer: extinguished,
rubble, impoverished,
sullen and reluctant.

2
Touch-me-not in the hand (yours)
is the message:
in its excitement it bursts,
its demise entwining things future.
The dark seeds want the earth.
What is going to happen?

3
No echo stirs,
the tongue is torn out,
the countering word ignored.
You keep the other cool –
but so much better would be screams
FROM YOU,
audible all the way here.

To whom?

Voice

What really is
is you, chosen by you
and your delight in hearing.
Sentences you discard,

making hills; you
give him vineyards
to hide in,
without you he could not
find his way back:
the nights are long,
aloneness is long.

You turn towns
into music, putrefaction
from strange windows
you blow away in rage.
Love was invented by you –
so strong, he is the only one
to whom it is denied.
The rift you made
out of life invents
hours early and late;
you have tried
to make age young,
pain tolerable;
the intolerable turns
to light in your eyes.
A shadow, you
enter poems, dragging

words towards you,
beauty. Of sharp claws
that entice us to either side

and deny admittance
you make the world, partly
for him, its co-inventor.

"That Mysterious Yearning toward the Chasm"

Whoever sees it sees life,
so it is written;
what is written, a torture to itself,
is what is least sure:
the beautiful, the pricked
heel, the hour
of Achilles' repose,
derided by tortoises.

Torn off veils
drying in the night breeze,
such are stars,
and our end comes far before theirs,
deriding ourselves
because of these riddles,
knotting our language,
when nothing needs to be said,
nothing needs to be seen.

It is acceptable
to bare one's head,
so that none of us may inflame the other
with our boldness,
to trust in our eyes and hearing
before other creatures
prove fitter,
having no fear of parting.

Immersed

She has the sound
she has taken from words;
this is arousal,
the act of writing,
reading music –

the sound disappears
into the world,
making its home in the rose hollow,
keeping his hands awake
for a game with the petals of roses;
the source picks up
such games
and rivers bring them back.

There stands death,
the proclaimer of endings,
blurred with lust,
soundless then
and with thorns parched.

Arguing with Parmenides

Incarcerated behind windows,
mistrustful doors,
hiding in order to be Seeming,
nothing, loyal to the unshakable
heart, peripheral, almost disowned.

The ribs resist,
the breath seeks a language
to utter the maxim of what is not:

that thoughts are the way,
that the hand-in-hand will be,
that chariot and mares are waiting,
that departure from one's dwelling
is separation.

Being is,
the sun rises from embraces,
light collides with light,
burning bushes, blossoming apple;
no dream batters us enough
for our losses.

Coming-to-be and passing away
close up the joints, the day is pure,
mutual effects rest,
the charioteer sleeps.

Explored in her eyes,
things undestroyed unfold;
nothing is mere name.

Song

Spread the word, save the visible,
that the mountain no longer be mountain,
that the flock of birds shatter.

Help to the eye: to blink,
like the shimmering above the grasses,
like the heart going to its death,
duration breaking.

But blossoms hurtle
in our faces, acacias
enchant the wind
and open wounds,
poppies, grow across the fields.

Tramping distance to pieces
is a soul's old song:
the silence at parting,
not knowing
a right way to say it –
coldly, angrily, resolved,
without paternal glory,
without.

How deeply it profits shame
to shelter a sentence from syllables.

You approach . . .

You approach,
wind buffeting your face,
trees in flight,
loyal envoys with birdsong.

Time is moved to interpret;
distance, the haze,
is agleam.
Likenesses
promise fortune,
tempering the indefinite.

Take the by-path, it is narrow.
Here is the impulse to touch.
Ours without exception.

Who is this departure meant for . . .

Who is this departure meant for,
this downward plunge into script?
So beautiful to read, so free
of grimy incomprehension,
of clueless divine judgements,
of parched eyesight.

To bring you here.
Madness enough awaits you;
tracked down
you are found producing books.
As in the beginning
as always.

The unsurpassable . . .

The unsurpassable,
if thereby truth be meant,
is music.
Walking the marches and scree
are part of it.

Its danger is beautiful,
its madness tranquil,
a grand
forest, felled by the storm.

Are you ready to be here,
protected by Parmenides' goddess?

Out of the lake the fountain . . .

Out of the lake the fountain
towers, wafting
gently back to the water
to end as spray.
Here vanishing is manifest:
it brings what lingers home.

I have brought fruit . . .

I have brought fruit
from the market,
meat and sweets:
they will heal our mouths.

Autumn bubbles
across the tables,
growth's ripening is fully done:
the message,
that abyss.

She stretches her life . . .

She stretches her life
to cover him;
light and shadow
we are,
deep, also fragile.

To be here
with a passion,
embraced by these fetters,
these boundaries.

These we keep.
We are condemned
to feel our bodies
like nothing else.

To live . . .

To live
without shame, in defiance,
as the crows do,
perpetually come home
to the fields,
horribly alike, black,
amassed to a threat,
a human face.

Overreach your outward gaze . . .

Overreach your outward gaze.
The lake below belongs to the mist
while distance already has the mountains.

The hands have won.
They arouse the waves
between their fingers.

The word glows
that means itself.
An urging, from where the sun is.
Warmth
engenders the senses.

Gentleness Paraphrases Itself

If the pull towards you
brings rain towards us
the flow will carry us along:
a redemption of feeling.

If arousal comes into its own
that path will open
that is more often taken in thought
than it demands.

With his whole body,
manifest as embracing,
someone writes down the story.

Intimations

Flies
whirr into sky blue.
Chestnut buds in their hundreds
promise you.

Bursting open they know
the blossom has begun
and that one change
holds all others within it,
adding future
to past.

The tree story
preserves its sentence.
Until the sun
sinks behind it.

This is the pain . . .

1
This is the pain
that makes it bearable
to stand here on nothing firm.

It turns to me
blindly distorting a word:
it is like your name.

2
This gives me the cue;
it stops the atomisation of days,
drawing me to the vineyard
where the ferment brims
and the wine clouds.

3
I followed it
day in, day out.
Nobody cared.
Dust enveloped my shoes.
Rain fell on the sorrow.

We have gazed ourselves free . . .

We have gazed ourselves free
of comparisons.
Frantic, she goes into hiding.
Pressing the senses
the hand hunts
the swelling,
fumbles with our parting.
The earth tastes of lust.
In this way love
shows forth in its images.

When I see her I know . . .

When I see her I know
my life is
a fleeting sketch,
grown old too late.

She stood at my heart
and struck with the blunt
edge of the axe.
"I can't split it".

Did she know the burning
petals behind the ribs?
"The old barrel is sore",
I thought, "this burning
is my final belonging."

The rage is dry.
Turning away grates.
Once my lips were as damp
as palms.

Result

To know that you are
exposed so utterly to what is lethal
in the other,
that you will lose him
in love,
fists pounding in your breast,
knowing it will
hit you,
that there is no other path
for the bullet,
and that you lie here, absurd,
excised
from the meeting
of day and night; but it is
a pleasure,
just as the void is a void.

When from the grey of the evening . . .

When from the grey of the evening
shadows reach into the poem
language turns
things towards us.
Like the snowfall, those first flakes . . .
you are caught up
in the turmoil.

The coat of mail, closeness . . .

The coat of mail, closeness,
is torn;
nakedness is only itself,
dead to me
its protection.

Far we went . . .

Far we went
walking behind ourselves.
In advance.

The sickness of the path
allotted us a place.

As if found again,
green-talking bushes,
the cock-crow
alerting us,
locking the door:

the beginning was untimely,
time since
has ensnarled itself
in the branches.

He sifted through himself . . .

He sifted through himself.
With him took
what things contained.

He left her,
created gardens,
never coming back
from their blossom.

Narrated into the poem . . .

Narrated into the poem:
the parched camellia twig.

It breaches the verses,
searches in the rubble
for the flower's end.

The words seek distance
from the lustre of the leaves,
their outlasting.

While changing . . .

While changing
from this train to the other
the picture faltered
and you unbuttoned
as if intending to stay.

For the length of a glance
the abyss was gone
along with our parting.

Two trains beside each other –
the fugue, her playing the piano
setting the trains in motion –
I remembered.

As if they were "parting
in peace".

Confined to their tracks:
the comforting simplicity
of parallels,
repose.

for Christiane

To wreak havoc as the clouds do . . .

To wreak havoc as the clouds do,
exploiting the wind
to transform themselves!

Your gaze leads you
far from being lasting;
left out
you walk on and on.

I kept . . .

I kept
her distance
and was close to her.

Conspicuous

Parting with our long wind
so pleasing to the alders.

On the banks of burns
clinging to golden rod
your tread has vanished,
ending as in dreams.

The track can be stopped.
The horizon
goes in pursuit.

She could have been wantonly gambled away,
sacrificed to the entrails,
severed.

Uplifted by writing . . .

Uplifted by writing,
high of head,
pushed out into human land,
to things,
so the burden for them is less.

On these things
lay your hand,
cover them with their skin
so they can feel themselves
and hear your breath:
be their evening light,
their lullaby,
comforted as you flag.

"It Rounds"

Since it has been
it returns
along the furrow

(the swathe of mist left behind),

its flowers
melting away.

Down from the hills
comes the gloaming.

Addressed by the wind . . .

Addressed by the wind
in the courtyards
of Mycenae.

The dust of ancient verse
runs to our ears,
and the song of the olive
rises from the haze below.

Their measure,
sunken in memory,
is forgotten.

For Hartmut Urban

You were missed on the platform.
I visited your grave.
On the language path to the colour path
we found each other again,
on the healing earth
of pictures past,
in the tempering black
of your colours.

Born in Brunnsee in the Austrian state of Styria in 1931, Alfred Kolleritsch studied History, German and Philosophy at the University of Graz, where, in 1964, he presented a doctoral thesis on the philosophy of Martin Heidegger. He taught at a grammar school in Graz from 1964 until 1993, and was a founder member of the Graz cultural centre 'Forum Stadtpark' in 1959, becoming its president in 1968, as well as a founder member of the Graz Authors' Association in 1973, to which he remained attached until 1983. He is editor of Austria's most influential literary magazine, *manuskripte*, which he co-founded in 1960. His own first work appeared in 1958, and he has since published poetry, as well as novels, film scripts, radio texts and children's books. His many poetry collections include the volumes *Augenlust* (Eyes' Desire, 1986), *Gegenwege* (Opposing Paths, 1991), *In den Tälern der Welt* (In the Valleys of the World, 1999), *Summe der Tage* (Sum of the Days, 2001), *Befreiung des Empfindens* (The Liberation of Feeling, 2004) and *tröstliche parallelen* (comforting parallels, 2006), and he has won several awards for his work, including the Petrarca Prize (1978), the Georg Trakl Prize (1987) and the Horst Bienek Prize for Poetry (2005).

Born in Glasgow in 1956, Iain Galbraith studied Modern Languages and Comparative Literature at the universities of Cambridge, Freiburg and Mainz, where he taught for several years. He is a widely-published translator of German-language writing, especially poetry, winning the John Dryden Prize for Literary Translation in 2004. His own poetry has appeared in anthologies and journals, including the *TLS*, *New Writing*, *PN Review* and *The Allotment: New Lyric Poets* (2006). Recent book publications include the poetry anthologies *Intime Weiten. XXV Schottische Gedichte* (2006) and *The Night Begins with a Question. XXV Austrian Poems 1978-2002* (2007), as well as a German edition of Michael Hamburger's prose writings, of which the first volume is *Pro Domo. Selbstauskünfte, Rückblicke und andere Prosa (2007)*.

www.ingramcontent.com/pod-product-compliance
Lightning Source LLC
Chambersburg PA
CBHW031158160426
43193CB00008B/425